T0031330

TO:

FROM:

LEAD LIKE A

COACH

HOW TO GET THE MOST SUCCESS OUT OF ANY TEAM

DR. KAREN MORLEY

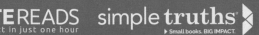

IGNITEREADS
spark impact in just one hour

simple truths®
Small books. BIG IMPACT.

Photo Credits
Internal images © end sheets, Anson_iStock/Getty Images, Volodymyr Kotoshchuk/Getty Images; page vi, Caiaimage/Tom Merton/Getty Images; page xii, jacoblund/Getty Images; page 9, andresr/Getty Images; page 10, 98, g-stockstudio/Getty Images; page 14, Thomas Barwick/Getty Images; page 20, 40, 68, 116, Westend61/Getty Images; page 32, Klaus Vedfelt/Getty Images; page 62, Carlina Teteris/Getty Images; page 74, 128, Hero Images/Getty Images; page 76, skynesher/Getty Images; page 78, 138, Peopleimages/Getty Images; page 88, recep-bg/Getty Images; page 92, Portra/Getty Images; page 108, Yuri_Arcuri/Getty Images; page 112, Luis Alvarez/Getty Images; page 137, fizkes/Getty Images Internal images on pages 19, 46, and 70 have been provided Unsplash; these images are licensed under CC0 Creative Commons and have been released by the author for use.

Published by Simple Truths, an imprint of Sourcebooks
P.O. Box 4410, Naperville, Illinois 60567-4410
(630) 961-3900
sourcebooks.com

Originally published as *Lead Like a Coach* in 2018 in Australia by Major Street Publishing.

Printed and bound in Singapore.
OGP 10 9 8 7 6 5 4 3 2 1

CONTENTS

iNTRODUCTiON

THE BEST LEADERS ARE ALSO COACHES

Everyone these days seems to need to get more done. The pace of life has increased, and we have much higher expectations of what we should do with our time.

After school, my step-grandson attends reading lessons and a raft of different activities. His social calendar is shockingly full too. We sometimes need to book three weeks in advance to spend a weekend afternoon with him—and he's only five and a half years old!

Expectations on all of us but especially on *leaders*

are increasing. Leaders are expected to get more done. They are expected to be available 24/7, to respond as if all information is always at their fingertips, and to work across multiple time zones.

In our twenty-first-century world of abundance, paradoxically, we seem to have fewer resources. We are captured by everyday pressures to do more, be more, know more...not to mention be more resilient and happier!

The challenges magnify further. Not only is it important to do more and be more, leaders need to help their team members to do the same. And that is no mean feat.

Many leaders I meet and coach feel these pressures like a weight on their shoulders. It's hard to be inspiring when you're weighed down by a heavy load.

The core proposition of this book is that leading like a coach will help you to lighten the burden you feel and give you more energy. By refocusing the way you engage with your team members, you can double their engagement and get more and better work done.

This book is for leaders who:

- care about the people they lead,
- care about their own success, and
- want to make a positive impact on their stakeholders, their families, and their communities.

Many leaders are still hesitant about coaching. They are not confident in their coaching ability.

Occasionally, a leader will confide in me that coaching feels risky. It feels as if you are giving up control. When you feel that you are under huge workload pressures, giving up control seems like the last thing you should do.

Underneath it all, there's a common fear that if your team does all the work—working at their maximum capability—what will you be doing? What will be your value? You are good at doing the work, you were promoted because you are, and now you have to stop doing the work. So what do you do?

You coach, of course!

PART 1

WHY YOU SHOULD COACH

1

ORGANIZATIONS ARE BETTER PLACES WHEN LEADERS COACH

Coaching, not controlling, is a compelling way for leaders to improve team performance. *Leaders who coach create and grow trust.* When trust is high, people are engaged and energized. They work harder for longer and are more productive.

Leaders are under great pressure to produce results at a faster pace using fewer resources where there are many more options to choose from. Unfortunately, most leaders react to this by adopting a command-and-control style of leadership. The pressure takes them over. They don't delegate enough, and they become overworked themselves and end up feeling overburdened. Teams disengage from leaders who control. Rather than increasing their performance, their work output falls and they become discouraged. Efforts by command-and-control leaders to produce more become counterproductive. Instead, they and their teams produce less and increase the risk of burnout.

Leaders who coach approach their responsibilities very differently. They focus on the team and how the team can be supported to produce better results. Rather than command and control, they develop and support.

Case Study: Letting Go of Control

Amy was invited to accept a senior leadership role for which she had no technical training. She took up the challenge, but she had doubts about her fit for the role—*and so did her team members*. They worked in security, and for many years, they hadn't seen much change in how they operated. The former manager had been a technical expert who had spent all his career in security. Amy's team members were all technical security experts.

About two years into the role, Amy was continuing to question whether this was a good fit for her. She felt that she needed to be tougher and more controlling and assert herself as the leader. She had a fairly blunt and direct style anyway, and she felt she needed to keep it ramped up.

Then, a critical incident happened. A large theft occurred in one of the regional teams. Amy worked with her regional manager and their team to deal with this. They followed the process and executed the response plan. But the HR team stepped in to challenge the way a particular staff member was dealt with. Rather than approaching the regional manager, HR came directly to Amy in head office.

Initially, Amy was ready to charge in to defend the actions of the regional manager as "the right thing to do."

From her point of view, things had gone very well.

The theft situation had been well controlled. She wanted to make sure that her team's actions were properly understood and they didn't experience blowback. She put on her armor to go into battle.

Luckily, we just happened to have a coaching session scheduled the morning prior to the showdown. The upshot of our coaching session was that Amy decided to reframe the intervention from HR. Rather than being something she needed to control, she saw it as an opportunity her team and HR could learn from. She saw that she needed to step out of the way for that to happen.

And she did. She told HR that she wouldn't be meeting with them but that her regional manager and his team would be. She spoke with her regional manager and told him what was happening and why. She spoke with the head of HR and asked that they do the same.

What Did Amy Do Differently?

Looking back at the case study, Amy learned a new way of dealing with a challenging situation. By letting go of control and trusting her regional manager to manage the internal fallout instead, she did several things.

1   Amy tried on a coaching cap. She redefined her role from manager to expert and let her regional manager be the expert in a situation that had occurred in his patch. She set out to coach him in how to manage the situation.

2   By setting up a learning frame, she focused attention on the future and what is possible rather than on the past and what was done. This enabled the focus of action to be on opportunities rather than mistakes.

3   She didn't use her power in a coercive way as she first intended to prove that her way was the right way. By stepping back, she showed trust in her regional manager by delegating responsibility back where it belonged.

Amy's mindset shifted to be more open. It was more collaborative and generous, thinking: How can we make this work? This event had unexpected follow-on benefits. Shifting to a coaching mindset meant Amy didn't have to be the security expert. She felt more congruent in her role as a coach. She could spend her time being more strategic and innovative rather than trying to learn a new functional skill—a skill that her team had in abundance.

She told her team her story of how she felt a lack of fit, why she was no longer going to try to fit, and why she valued their technical skills. Her relationships with her team members became deeper. She showed greater trust in the team (and herself) by delegating more to them. The team has repaid that by generating more ideas, making more suggestions, and taking more leadership actions. Amy continues to take a coaching rather than a controlling stance, and this is spreading out to other stakeholders in the business.

She's living the differences between a commanding, directive culture and an empowering, coaching culture (see Figure 1.1 below). She's feeling more congruent, growing relationships that are more positive, and giving herself space to sweat the big stuff.

Figure 1.1: Command-and-Control vs. Coaching Leadership Styles

	COMMANDING CULTURE	COACHING CULTURE
ROLE	Manager as expert	Person as expert on self
TIME	The past: what holds me back?	The future: what propels me forward?
ACTIONS	Mistakes: what went wrong?	Opportunities: what do we need/want?
POWER	Coercion: do it my way	Attraction: how will you do it?
MINDSET	Show me how it will work	How can we make this work?

It's clear that coaching produces better results than a command-and-control leadership style. Yet the command-and-control style continues to be used. Why? *Because coaching goes against the grain for many leaders.* While 80 percent of organizations say they are keen to develop a coaching culture, a coaching style goes against the grain for many of them too. They continue to reward command-and-control styles. A core proposition of command-and-control is that the people at the top make the decisions and others aren't to be trusted. This is just bad for business.

The key reasons that leaders like Amy don't coach more is they are:

- captured by everyday pressures to produce results,
- not confident in their coaching capability, and
- unclear or unaware of the connection between coaching, team engagement, and productivity.

If you coach more, you will create a workplace that everyone enjoys more. ***Bad bosses are the single biggest reason people leave organizations. Great bosses are the single biggest reason people stay in organizations.***

ACTIVITY

1. Review how empowered your team members feel. How actively engaged are your team members?

2. What improvement would you like to see in the engagement of your team?

COACHING IS CONTAGIOUS

Any time someone is coached well, they become more coach-like themselves. This is what I call *the contagion effect*. When you coach people in your organization, they begin to find their own answers and become more resourceful. People work more effectively together because they engage in dialogue. They listen and ask questions rather than tell others what to do. They see resistance as an opportunity to explore other perspectives rather than as a threat. The nature of conversations between people changes. Interactions become more positive. The coaching style spreads as more people enjoy its experience.

The contagion effect of coaching means that the efforts of each leader are magnified through the efforts of everyone they coach.

Case Study: Coaching to Develop Your Team

Jackie, leader of the marketing group at Next Jump, received feedback that she was seen as putting herself first. It was preventing her from being offered leadership opportunities. She acknowledged that she put her own success ahead of the success of others. She was on a quest to get to the top. She couldn't see any other way to do it.

It took some getting used to, but once Jackie realized that her behavior was limiting her aspirations, she worked out a plan for change. She started by coaching once a month with the deliberate intention of helping others to be successful. That was a challenge, but she stuck with it. She started coaching more frequently—weekly, then daily.

After about a year, the feedback she received changed remarkably. Others around her were developing, and she could see the benefits of her shift in leadership style spreading across the business.

She had thought that if she spent so much time coaching, she wouldn't be able to get her job done. If she spent her time on others, she wouldn't be successful.

But what Jackie has realized is that she can be successful in a completely different way. When leaders coach, they create a culture that is *empowering* and *energizing*.

When Leaders Coach, the Benefits Spread

Jackie's organization in the case study above makes it a priority that each person must be counted on to help others succeed. They deliberately embrace the coaching ripple effect.

By being deliberately developmental, a coaching culture empowers and develops current leaders. At the same time, it grows future leaders.

What is evident in Jackie's story is the shift from an individual to a collective benefit. She was a commanding, controlling boss. It took great effort for her to switch from being a controller to a coach. She stopped asking, "How can I be my best?" Instead, she asked, "How can I help my team be its best?"

Leaders who coach ask:

- "How can I help my team be its best?" rather than command
- "How do I help the teams I am a part of to best meet our challenges?" rather than compete
- "How do I balance an investment in future capability with a focus on results right now?" rather than control

Leaders who coach cultivate trust by supporting and developing others. They do what they can to equip others to do their best work. Not only does more work of a better quality get done, it has the enormous benefit of relieving the "power stress" that leaders feel. While Jackie continues to work on her coaching skills, the rewards of her new leadership style are tangible. She doesn't have to fear failure as she previously did.

HOW COACHING REALIZES POTENTIAL

By focusing on the future, leaders give others the opportunity to imagine the future. Rather than being stale, set, or safe, *coaching* opens up limitless possibilities to grow talents and skills to their full potential. Figure 2.1 highlights the distinctions between a future-oriented rather than a backward-looking focus and between a controlling and a coaching approach.

Figure 2.1: Future-Oriented Coaching vs. Backward-Looking Control

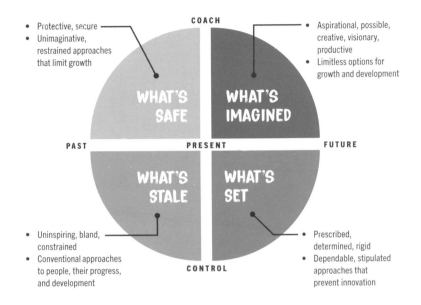

A controlling style that focuses on the past is stale and out of date. It constrains growth and holds back development. A controlling style that is future-focused helps to grow capabilities, but by being fixed on set responses—the tried and true—it limits innovation and autonomy.

A coaching approach that is based on the past is highly protective. It may feel safe, but with its protective, cocoon-like wrapping, growth and innovation are suppressed.

A coaching approach that is future-oriented gives the person you are coaching the opportunity to generate their own options for growth. They can pursue what they can imagine. It offers the greatest promise to fulfil their potential.

When leaders practice future-oriented coaching, they are opening the door to team members' aspirations, creating the opportunity for them to grow and develop to the greatest extent possible.

It's not just team members who benefit when leaders coach. Leaders also benefit when they coach. The action of coaching itself becomes rewarding. Rather than telling others what you already know, you hear others' interpretations and the decisions they make. By developing others, leaders are also developing themselves.

ACTIVITY

1. How well do you balance your attention between future capability needs versus results right now?

2. What might you do to get the balance right?

3. What percentage of your time is focused on skills needed in the past rather than skills needed for the future?

4. Is your focus sufficiently aspirational and motivational for your team?

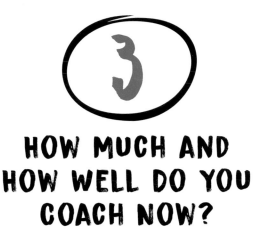

HOW MUCH AND
HOW WELL DO YOU
COACH NOW?

Having set the field of play for coaching, it's now time for tryouts. What is your coaching capability right now? How do you rate your coaching skills?

To help you assess your capability and focus your development, I'll introduce you to three models I regularly use when I coach. They are:

1 The **why**: a framework to understand how adults develop.

2   The **what**: a continuum to focus your development.

3   The **how**: a scoreboard to help chart the course of your development as a coach.

THE WHY: A FRAMEWORK TO UNDERSTAND HOW ADULTS DEVELOP

Having greater insight into how adult learning occurs will maximize your own learning. You will be better able to support others as they learn.

How do you see your own development to date? What is your appetite for authority and the challenges of leading others?

Being responsible for a team that achieves results is very different from being an individual contributor. To be a good leader, you need to be comfortable exercising authority. As you move into roles that are bigger and give you more responsibility, you need to adapt the way you see yourself, and you need to adapt the way you value the work you do.

Adult development and exercising authority are closely linked. Exercising authority effectively means being able to see things from many perspectives. Responsibility for resources and making decisions is easier if you see multiple ways of doing things. You don't have to give up your own position to do this. You can understand the views and opinions of others as you strengthen or clarify your own.

Coaching means taking multiple perspectives without necessarily advocating one over the others. It requires listening and patience. It requires the ability to separate you as subject from you as object. The ability to take an objective, detached perspective on how you enact your role and how you engage with your team members will help you to coach.

Case Study: Questioning Authority

When I met with Tom to begin our coaching program, he was struggling with his own sense of leadership identity. His coaching program began with this statement: "I know my strengths. I'm very good at managing relationships and being collaborative and at thinking strategically. I know that I overplay my strengths and that I keep relying on them to avoid the business/management stuff. I question deeply what authority is and feel challenged by it."

For Tom, authority was tightly bound with status, management, and execution. He viewed all of these negatively. We agreed that a key goal of coaching would be to work out how to challenge his perspective that authority and warmth were contradictory.

Tom labeled a prominent organizational leader as insincere. This was someone who excelled on the execution side. Tom identified that this was part of his struggle with authority. What he realized he was doing was conflating execution, status, and insincerity. He really didn't want to be like this person whose behavior he viewed as distasteful.

Tom avoided directing his team to get things done because he valued having friendly relationships with his team. He thought that a drive to execute meant that he couldn't have friendly relationships with them. On reflection, he was able to articulate that what sat underneath this was his self-image as likable. Likability and authority didn't go together.

Being likable was mixed up with being warm and having good emotional intelligence. Tom was praised for his self-awareness and his ability to read the emotions and dynamics of others around him.

He was struggling to see how it was possible to be an authoritative leader and a "nice person." Exploring options for how to use his warmth and emotional intelligence to be authoritative helped Tom to imagine how he could be both. He came to see how to be authoritative without having to be friends.

One of the challenging pieces of feedback from

his boss was how Tom shared information. Because he viewed himself as friendly and approachable, he shared information widely. He regularly spoke with a variety of people across the organization to share the latest news. Tom enjoyed this engagement and the sense of power that came from passing on the news that others didn't have access to.

What Tom *hadn't* realized was that this behavior was compromising the way he was seen by important superiors.

The shock associated with this feedback was helpful for Tom to reframe the relationships that were important to him and why. He was able to identify that his need for warmth and friendliness was misfiring. He had to own up to his own status and power needs here: what he saw as his source of power—providing information to others—was a way of maintaining his status. He not only hadn't labeled it that way, he hadn't realized that it was counterproductive.

Realigning Values

As the case study shows, viewing authority as different from status opens up the idea that it could come from willingness to self-authorize. Tom realized that he'd mixed up his ideals. He could be much less friendly yet still be warm and engaging. Giving up the need to be friends meant more opportunity to take up authority, and he could exercise his authority in a way that was congruent with the leader he wanted to be.

Tom reflected on what had changed. "I had some breakthrough thinking. I was not allowing myself to get comfortable with exercising my authority. I was still wanting to be friends. I was wanting to 'not be like x,' and that, I can see now, just seems to be backward thinking. Some unconscious things have been released about my relationship to authority. I can engage in a much clearer way; I'm calling people out. Having a strong focus on accountability and execution means that I've given myself authority to move into this space. I'm holding boundaries in a much more overt way. I am stepping in and being authoritative. I can do this and maintain my warmth. And I don't have to worry about whether anyone likes me. In fact, I've improved the trust that people have in me, and that is more important. *This is a better me, and I want to be known for it.*"

Through coaching, we were able to get a better view on whose perspectives Tom was taking. Coaching continued Tom's development from the socialized to the self-authoring form of mind. Reacting against the authority figure he didn't like kept him bound by that perspective on authority. Letting go of the resistance helped him develop a more congruent sense of his own authority. Coaching helped his thinking become more flexible. He was able to take multiple perspectives openly without feeling internal conflict.

ACTIVITY

1. How easy do you find it to take the perspectives of others?

2. What is your own comfort level with exercising your own authority? Where do you experience limits to how you exercise authority?

3. What space do you leave your team to act on their own authority?

4. What connection, if any, can you see between your comfort level and the space you leave your team?

THE WHAT: A CONTINUUM TO FOCUS YOUR DEVELOPMENT

The Know, Do, Believe, Be continuum (see Figure 3.1) offers a practical way of deciding what to develop.

The logic is that learning starts with knowledge. You've probably devoted a lot of your development time to knowing your area of technical expertise. Once you know how to do something, you build your expertise through practice. You build mastery in particular skills.

Figure 3.1: The Know, Do, Believe, Be Continuum

Beliefs or mindsets play a role in learning. How do your beliefs affect what you learn and develop mastery in? What do you believe about what leadership or coaching is?

These then build to being. This level of learning is associated with identity—who you are and who you want to become. When your knowledge, skills, and beliefs are congruent with your sense of identity, you have achieved the desired state of unconscious competence.

Turns in the leadership pipeline mean that different knowledge, skills, and attitudes are required at different stages of your development. As you move into more senior leadership roles, your identity may need to adapt for you to be successful. If your sense of identity is very strong, you may find it more difficult to imagine yourself as suitable for some roles. Alternatively, you may find it more difficult to adapt into them.

ACTIVITY

1. **What do you need to know to improve your coaching?**

2. **What skills do you have, and what do you need to learn so that you "do" coaching?**

3. **What do you or don't you believe about coaching?**

4. **What have you already mastered? What does it mean to you to be a coach?**

KNOW HOW TO COACH

Where do you start? Do you know how to coach but are not sure about when to coach? Are you coaching everyone or just some team members? Do you focus on strengths as well as deficits? Is your coaching limited to team members, or do you use your coaching style with peers and other stakeholders?

Knowing how to coach, when to coach, and who to coach is a good starting point. Two key issues to bear in mind are:

1   **Beware cognitive overload.** Many leaders experience cognitive overload in their day-to-day work. A busy workload plus a learning program increases the degree of difficulty. Work through these activities in smaller chunks rather than large ones. Use your calendar so that you remind yourself to participate in small learning acts at regular intervals. Use the reminders to keep your momentum going. This will help you learn more and retain your new knowledge and skills.

2   **Separate coaching from performance management.** Distinguish coaching from performance management as far as possible. There are multiple opportunities for coaching. Use coaching skills to help reduce the threat and negativity of performance management–based activities. You will be more receptive to finding opportunities to coach, and your team will be more receptive to being coached.

Keep your focus on the positive. If you associate coaching with positive experiences, it will strengthen your resolve to coach.

Corridor conversations, micro-coaching conversations, and collaborative discussions are all great options for coaching. Focus on ensuring quality conversations, which better align with a coaching culture. This will also provide a positive experience to the person being coached.

DO COACHING

Practice coaching behaviors and conversations, as this grows mastery and confidence. Practice, practice, practice. To avoid the perception that coaching employees is risky, create opportunities for practice. Get feedback from trusted peers if you can. Find opportunity for reflection and refinement of your own practice of coaching.

Be coached. When leaders themselves are coached,

the likelihood that they will coach others increases. It also increases the support they provide to their teams. They delegate more, micromanage less, pay more attention to employees' developmental needs, and put effort into creating a positive and engaging work environment. Reciprocal coaching between peers who are learning together is a powerful way to embed learning into practice. Who might you partner up with?

BELIEVE IN COACHING

You've probably made it to this point in this book because you have some level of belief in the value of coaching. What are your unanswered questions about its value? *A coaching style won't be right for every situation. But it's right for more situations than you think.*

Keep your learning focused on what's relevant to you. How does it help you do your work? Use it to gain insight into the challenges you face. How might coaching help you achieve a goal? This leads to new perspectives and solutions, which is energizing.

KNOW AND TRANSITION YOUR LEADERSHIP IDENTITY TO "COACH"

It might seem like a big shift to grow your coaching style to be a key part of how you engage with your team. With that shift comes uncertainty, which is just the opposite of what you want to feel. As the leader, you're meant to be certain, right?

To make a successful leadership identity transition to coach will take a fine balance. Balancing the certainty you have as a leader with the confusion you have of letting go may be a challenge.

During this time, how you see yourself is changing. It might feel a bit like you are in a hall of mirrors. It's as if there is a variety of different mirrors that distort the way you look, making you appear in different ways depending on where you look. In some mirrors, you loom large; in others, you are small; and in yet others, you seem to disappear. The different reflections are all you yet not you as you transition.

It's normal to feel this wobbliness and distortion. That's part of the process. Figure 3.2 shows the relationships between certainty, confusion, and clarity as you transition your identity.

Figure 3.2: How to Transition Your Leadership Identity

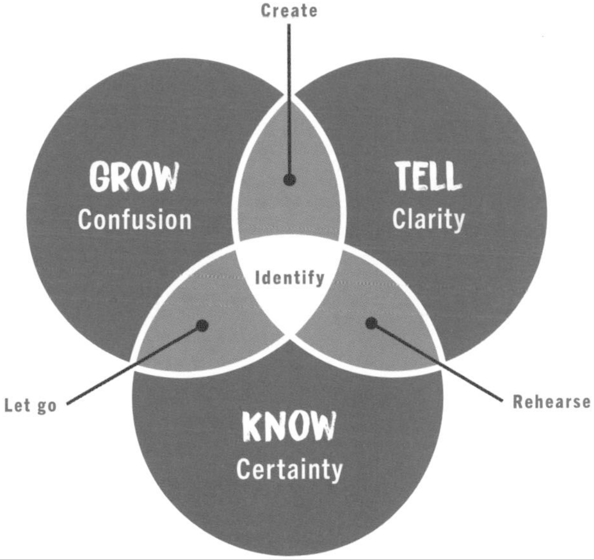

Create

GROW
Confusion

TELL
Clarity

Identify

Let go

KNOW
Certainty

Rehearse

LEADERSHIP TRANSITIONS WILL CREATE A SENSE OF CONFUSION

Clarity about who you are is disturbed as new challenges arise and different responses are needed. Your identity may be stretched and challenged and that causes the confusion. Your old certainties just aren't as helpful as they used to be. It helps to let go of the need to be certain if you are to learn how to "be a new me" in your new context.

It's natural to prefer to have certainty and to know who we are. To grow, we need to let go of that certainty, but that means experiencing confusion and uncertainty for a period. Through the confusion and the exploration of new ideas and behaviors, we begin to create a new sense of identity.

PART 2

GET READY TO COACH

DEVELOP YOUR COACHING PRESENCE

Coaching is generative. It focuses on how to develop new capabilities, see new horizons, and create new opportunities. Outstanding leaders begin with the ideal of generativity. This is the attitude of creating, generating, and producing. Their key question is, "How can I grow this person's competence in a way that is respectful and effective?"

LONG-TERM EXCELLENT PERFORMANCE

When you focus on long-term excellent performance, not just short-term gains, your focus shifts from *"What work needs to get done?"* to *"What capabilities does this person need to develop to get this job done?"*

One of the simplest ways to do this is to avoid answering when a team member seeks advice. For example, they may ask you "What do you think?" or "What's my next step?" Instead of answering, the coaching trick is to ask a question back, for example, "What have you thought of?" or "What do you think your next step should be?"

Leaders are primed to know the answer and to respond as quickly as they can. Resisting the temptation to do so can be hard! In fact, what I have observed when training leaders in coaching skills is that the challenge is often just to notice that this is happening. Then they can use it as an opportunity. Answering questions is pretty much instinctive. To stop and respond differently takes mindful attention and effort.

You may eventually need to answer the question because your team member just doesn't know. But at least 99 percent of the time, they either already do know the right answer, or you can help shape their thinking in the right direction in order to enable them to find the answer for themselves.

Case Study: Moving from a Directive to a Coaching Style of Leadership

Jack had a goal to change his leadership style. He wanted to reduce the amount of time he was in directive mode and increase his use of coaching. He had transitioned into a role where he was now a manager of managers. He realized that he had to change his style to meet the workload demands of the new role. He could not continue to be the expert on *everything* in his group, nor could he know *all* the details of a project as he had in his previous role.

He started answering questions with questions rather than giving answers. He started one-on-one meetings by asking his team members what was on their minds. He asked them what they wanted to achieve in the meeting rather than hitting them with a list of demands for information or action. This was starting to shift the quality of Jack's relationships with his team. He felt very encouraged by the positive responses from most of them and the relief from not having the pressure to know everything. The changes were almost a complete success.

Almost.

Jack was frustrated by one of his team members, Dan, who often came to him for advice and approval. While Jack's behavior had changed, Dan's hadn't.

Dan was quiet and self-confessedly rules-oriented. He didn't show a great deal of initiative, yet he could be relied on to do his work well and to help other team members when they reached out to him. People trusted him. Having been in his role for about eight years, he was seen as the corporate memory of the team.

Jack realized that to shift Dan's behavior with him, he needed to help Dan achieve greater insight into his behavior and style. He realized that there was quite a good fit between his former directive style and the way Dan preferred to be managed. This was making it harder to create change. Jack realized he couldn't just change what he did and expect that Dan would change too.

Jack became more open and explicit with his team about his development. He shared with them what he aimed to do and how he was doing it. With Dan, he spoke about his changing views on authority and leadership. He shared information on habits of mind with Dan. He invited Dan to reflect on his own development and how he saw authority.

Jack bit the bullet and began to provide more feedback to Dan on how he experienced his behaviors. He used this as a way to begin a discussion about

what other behaviors Dan could try. It was a challenge. Jack realized that when he was in coaching mode, it wasn't his role to tell Dan what style he should adopt. He needed to open him up to the variety of style possibilities and allow Dan to choose.

Jack initially self-assessed as being controlling on the Coaching Mindset continuum (see Figure 4.1 below). Autocratic and controlling mindsets shut people down. They are not generative and become

self-defeating rather than self-generating. A supportive mindset begins and a benevolent mindset acceler-
ates the movement to generativity. The pinnacle of a
generative approach is coaching. Jack thought that he
was somewhere between supportive and benevolent.
His aspiration is to get to coaching. He wants to be
seen as a leader who is a coach and is recognized by
others for his coaching style.

Figure 4.1: The Coaching
Mindset Continuum

AUTOCRATIC CONTROLLING SUPPORTIVE BENEVOLENT COACHING

Jack was inspired by Michelangelo, who said, "I saw
the angel in the marble and carved until I set him free."
A coaching mindset looks for the angel in the marble.
It looks for the potential within each team member and
then works to help it be realized.

ACTIVITY

1. **What is your usual mindset?**

AUTOCRATIC	CONTROLLING	SUPPORTIVE	BENEVOLENT	COACHING

2. **What might you do to move closer to or maintain a coaching mindset?**

3. **What long-term focus on excellent performance do you need to have?**

4. **How might you enable self-correction (to improve each team member's insight into their patterns and style and the ability to see their actions objectively)?**

5. **What can you do to support self-generation (to develop each team member's capability to renew, ask questions, and let go of unhelpful assumptions)?**

TURNING YOUR COACHING MINDSET INTO ACTION

To be like a coach, you need to have a coaching presence. This is how you turn the coaching mindset into action. The mindset is that you actively seek to find and help to realize the potential in others. To do this, you show them your vulnerability, empathy, humility, and appreciation (see Figure 4.2).

Imagine a lake at dawn when it is calm and still. Imagine the surface of the lake is like a millpond or a mirror. The peaceful reflectiveness that it evokes is like a lure. It is as if the world is taking a deep breath. It is an invitation to pause, to sit still and just be. This is an important part of what a coaching presence should be like: calm, still, an invitation.

When you are vulnerable, you show up as your full self. You don't have all the answers, and this offers an invitation to the person you are coaching to mirror you. Warmth and empathy make the connection personal and meaningful.

Figure 4.2: Elements of Coaching Presence

A coach is humble, comfortable asking questions rather than having the answers. This supports the desire to offer, to give, rather than to take.

By being generous with appreciation, a coaching presence helps others find their motivation to achieve their goals and to continue to develop.

Coaching presence is an offer of recognition, understanding, connection, and subjectivity.

Be Vulnerable While Coaching to Increase Your Connection

If you allow yourself to be vulnerable, you will increase personal connection with others in your team. Open yourself to the coaching relationship by giving up your expert/hierarchical power, and show up as the real you.

Being vulnerable is like being on a suspension bridge. You need to be open to the drop, the sway, and bounce of the bridge. All the while, you stay confident the bridge will hold you and you will successfully cross to the other side.

Leadership and vulnerability go hand in hand. Being vulnerable means taking the risk to make connections with others despite the sways and bounces of interpersonal interactions. It's the ability to stay confident. It is essential for being accessible to your team and other stakeholders.

Figure 4.3 is the vulnerability matrix. As you can see, if you are low in openness, then you will be either guarded or protective in your relationships. If you are high in openness but low in risk, it's like being on a low bridge over an empty stream—it doesn't necessarily advance the relationship.

Figure 4.3: How to Be Vulnerable

Brené Brown emphasizes the importance of vulnerability to meaningful human relationships. Her view of vulnerability is that it is a sign of courage, not weakness. Vulnerability builds human connection, and that's what gives meaning and purpose to our lives. Through your vulnerability as coach, you offer connection. You increase your team's opportunity for finding greater meaning and purpose at work.

It takes courage to risk vulnerability. The suggestion here is not to suddenly start disclosing highly personal information. You should not take yourself out on suspension bridges that are too flimsy or poorly anchored. Read the context with care. While sharing vulnerability builds enormous trust between people, there needs to be a foundation of trust already. Who do you trust? Who could you trust more than you currently do? How might you explain more about yourself to others to let them know more about you as a person, your values and aspirations? Start in small ways with what feels reasonably comfortable, then experiment and expand. This is where I invoke the Goldilocks rule: not too much discomfort, not too little, *just the right amount*.

Sometimes, people confuse vulnerability with weakness. Increased disclosure about your values, motives, reflections, and perspectives—your own story—demonstrates strength. It builds trust and is generally very inspiring.

Use Your Empathy to Honor the Feelings of Others

Connecting with people is fundamental to leading them. Your offer of vulnerability starts the process. Next, use your empathy to engage with the other person's experiences and feelings.

Empathy can be lost in the daily pressures of work. There are many distractions, and your attention can be fractured as it is pulled in many directions. To coach, it helps if you can put yourself into the context of the other person and pay attention to them and their experiences. Try to honor their experiences and feelings. Figure 4.4 shows the impact you have on your relationships depending on the perspective you take and your level of emotional awareness. If you stay with your own perspective, you will disconnect from or avoid the feelings of others. If you take the other person's perspective, you will *at least* recognize their feelings.

Figure 4.4: How to Create Empathy

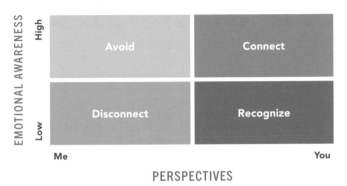

Empathy grows from your ability to take the other person's perspective and have a high level of emotional awareness that allows you to connect with them on a human level.

Empathy is a human superpower. It reduces social and power distance, overcomes differences between people, and provokes social change. It is vital to any coaching relationship.

Daniel Goleman speaks of three kinds of empathy as important for leaders. They are:

1 **Cognitive empathy:** being able to take another person's perspective and to gain a sense of how they are feeling.

2 **Emotional empathy:** being able to feel what another person feels. To do this, you need to read the other person's signals, then generate an awareness of what they might be feeling and recall your own experience of that emotion.

3 **Empathic concern:** being able to sense what the other person might need from you. This means weighing up the strength of the feeling and responding with compassion.

A challenge for leaders is that they generally place themselves at a higher rung on the social ladder. Hierarchical status helps them project themselves onto the top rungs. But that means they pay less attention to others. To manage expectations and the demand on their time, leaders become less socially responsive to others, and they tune in less. This in turn lowers empathy. How does this impact you?

Coaching is an opportunity. Coaching invites you to pay more attention to your team members, to tune in to them emotionally, and to connect. When people feel listened to and know that they matter, they are more motivated.

A Humble, Curious Stance Lets Others Be Their Best

Coaching is built on asking questions and avoiding telling the solution. We are predisposed to *tell* others what we know rather than to *ask* what they know. Leaders in particular fall prey to this tendency. Leaders often feel as if they are on a hurtling express train, so sure of their destination, focused only on getting there, on being on time. Relationships, however, need stops along the way. They need curiosity and pauses, and you need to devote time to them. Relationships need reciprocal two-way interaction. They need the slower train, the cadence of asking as well as telling, if they are to flourish.

As the leader-coach, you don't have to be the expert. You can step back from being in telling mode. You're not the expert on the other person. As Figure 4.5 shows, when your curiosity is low and you know the answer, you are most likely to tell. Instead, allow the other person to be the expert on themselves. Switch to high curiosity: ask them. You lead them to find the right answer.

When the answer is unknown or uncertain, if you engage with low curiosity, you will avoid finding out what is possible or known by others. If you engage with high curiosity—and ask—you find new solutions. A side benefit of a coaching relationship is that you learn too; you learn as much as the person you are coaching.

Figure 4.5: How to Be Humble

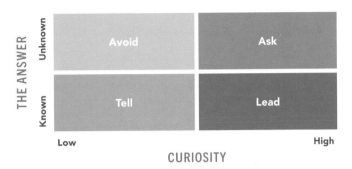

What remains difficult in some organizations is for junior staff to feel safe to bring up a range of issues that need to be addressed. They have information that might reduce accidents and injuries in the workplace and mistakes that might detract from value for customers, but they are unwilling to say as much. A coaching climate is more likely to create a level of safety for everyone to share information and communicate. It relies on the leader being humble, having the ability to listen carefully, and being less certain of having all the answers. When a leader behaves like this, staff are more likely to make out-of-the-box suggestions and to volunteer contentious information. Such an environment is rarely built where leaders do the bulk of the telling.

How to Take Your Humility into a Coaching Conversation

Coaching means making the shift from telling—the hallmark of the manager—to asking, which is the hallmark of the coach. You can see a conversation as being like an artist's palette. In your conversation, spread out all the colors on your palette. Choose and mix the different colors into your conversation. This gives it greater light and shade, greater appeal.

Balancing asking with telling on your palette can be difficult to achieve. Asking when you know or believe you know can be especially challenging. To improve your asking skills, try using these prompts:

- What leads you to conclude that?
- What data do you have for that?

- ► What causes you to say that?

- ► Help me understand your thinking.

- ► What is the significance of that?

- ► How does this relate to your concerns?

- ► Where does your reasoning go next?

- ► How would your proposal affect…?

- ► What is this like?

Appreciate Others to Let Them Know They Matter

Appreciation lets us know that what we do matters. Knowing that we matter connects us to others. When we feel that what we do at work is valuable, it satisfies one of our deepest human needs. *Appreciation tells people that they are valued.* Appreciation grows satisfaction, which increases performance and results in people feeling valued, as depicted in this graphic.

| Appreciation | Satisfaction | Performance | Value |

Not enough time is spent letting people know that what they do matters, that they make a contribution that has value, and that they are worthy of being noticed. We spend too much time at work for our contribution to go underrecognized.

I commonly hear this phrase: "You can expect to hear about it if there's a problem." Sometimes, it seems as if there is almost an *aversion* to saying positive things about others. It makes sense that many of us are averse to conflict. It is negative, it can be difficult and uncomfortable, and we may fear its potential to disrupt relationships.

It is more puzzling that we undercommunicate positive admiration and appreciation toward others. What a paradox this is: feeling appreciated is something that is so fundamental to our well-being, but so few of us go out of our way to make others feel appreciated. How can we break the pattern?

STEP 1: TUNE INTO ACTIONS THAT ARE WORTH APPRECIATING

You need to set aside your own busyness, be mindful, and pay attention to others. What you notice when you do this doesn't have to be a huge event or something even moderately life-changing. It might be a regular, day-to-day occurrence that seems pretty insignificant, but it makes a small difference to how your hour or your day goes. Notice what you can.

STEP 2: PROVIDE APPRECIATION

Let's focus on giving high-value appreciation. Take thirty seconds to think about a recent experience you have of a team member's behavior. Imagine that you are going to express your appreciation to this person in an upcoming conversation or meeting. Write down what you would say to them.

How specific is it? We are often general rather than specific. We talk about how we felt rather than what was done that caused us to feel great. For example, "You gave a great presentation to the client yesterday."

The initial response will be to feel good. Yet what was done that was great? You might infer that what you did was due to something entirely different from what others noticed or what was actually appreciated.

Be specific about why you thought the presentation was great. This is as valuable for the person you are appreciating as it is for you. Do you appreciate it when someone completes tasks before they are due or when they contribute a new idea? What's the pattern to what you notice and appreciate? How balanced are you? As a leader, you direct particular actions by your pattern of appreciation. Does your pattern mean that you over- or underappreciate particular behaviors or particular people? What's the balance of your appreciation?

Avoid attribution when you express your appreciation. Appreciation that attributes value to certain personality characteristics tends to box the person in, and you may get your attributions wrong. What could be wrong with saying to someone "you have such a great sense of humor"? Perhaps they believe they have a great sense of humor, but perhaps they don't. Perhaps they value humor, but perhaps not. Perhaps they don't want to be seen as the joker, and they would prefer to be taken seriously. In that moment, being told by you what they "are" could feel limiting. And if that's repeated over time, the attribution may become unhelpful.

"You" statements tend to provoke a reaction, sometimes even defensiveness. "I" statements that focus on my own experience of your behavior don't. "I enjoyed your comment. It was very helpful because it relieved some of the tension that was building up. Our conversation was becoming very intense, and it felt like we were stalling. What you said helped us to lift our heads a bit and go back into the conversation with more energy and a different focus. We were able to move forward." This approach works equally well for positive and negative statements.

Appreciation that is about the experience of what

you have done rather than an attribution of what you are has the greatest value. When I know how you experience what I do, I will feel most valued.

STEP 3: MAKE IT A HABIT

Incorporate appreciation into your coaching style and help others feel good about the contribution they make. *Help them thrive.*

Coaching presence is based on vulnerability, empathy, humility, and appreciation. To be like a coach, identify your strengths and the areas you need to develop. What do you need to improve to have a coaching mindset and bring out the full potential of your team and each member of it?

BELIEVE IN YOUR POWER TO COACH

Being a better coach means setting aside the need to be an *individual* contributor. It means leaving behind the control and status of management to focus on being the leader of the team. With a coaching mindset, your focus is to enable the team and each individual team member to grow to their full potential. *That's your most important contribution.*

COACH THE PERSON, NOT THE PROBLEM

When you're playing football, to play well you need to keep your eye on the ball. Where the ball is and what's happening to it helps you identify what the next play should be. In coaching, keeping your eye on the ball translates to keeping your eye on the person, *not their problem*.

Coaching is not about solving someone's problem for them but helping them to be able to solve their own problems. First, when you coach, you need to understand the person's context (see Figure 5.1). You need to hear how they construct and make sense of their problem.

Figure 5.1: The Coaching Focus

In between the problem and you, there's the coachee. Listen deeply to what the coachee says about the problem. Avoid offering advice and suggestions. Ask how they see their problem. What have they tried to do about their problem? Where are they stuck? Is this where they always get stuck? What's the barrier to finding their own solution?

Most leaders find it hard to avoid automatically naming the solution. Your task as coach is not to find the solution. You might already know the solution—or at least some options—but hold back and help the person find their own.

STOP MANAGING, START COACHING

Be clear about the distinction between coaching and other forms of engagement. Coaching requires a different focus and use of power. Be clear about these distinctions to make it easier to coach (see Figure 5.2).

Figure 5.2: Differences between Coaching, Mentoring, Managing, and Consulting

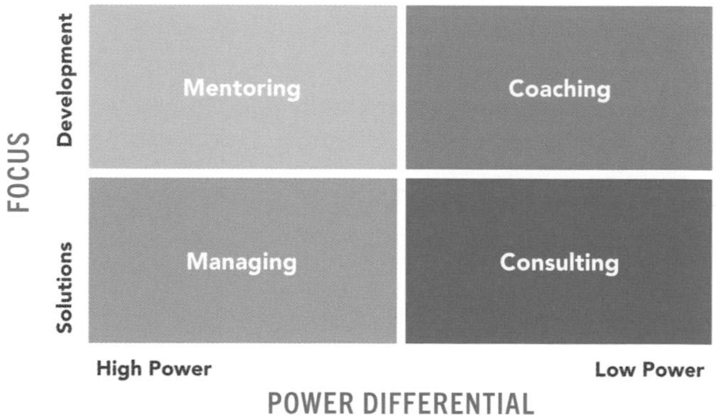

FOCUS

Development

Mentoring

Coaching

Solutions

Managing

Consulting

High Power

Low Power

POWER DIFFERENTIAL

Coaching is the leadership mode that puts others first. This makes it different from managing, consulting, and mentoring. They are all legitimate ways of engaging. Each engages power differently and has a different focus for the interaction.

Mentoring is development-focused, like coaching, but there is a bigger difference between the mentor's and the individual's expertise. Both managing and consulting are solutions-focused.

Coaching reduces the power differential and focuses on development, not solutions. It's not just external coaches who coach, and it's not just leaders who coach. It's a style of engaging that anyone might use.

Team members might coach one another, and they might coach their boss as well as be coached by him or her. To transition between the different styles, prime yourself to put on a different cap. The metaphorical cap reminds you to adjust the power differential and your focus.

ACTIVITY

1. Mentor, coach, manager, consultant: which is your default mode?

2. How focused are you on solutions (rather than development) with team members?

3. Dial your power down. Use a metaphor like a coaching cap as a way to prime yourself before you coach. How will you prime yourself to take a coaching approach?

4. What support or challenge can you give right now that will help your team members develop their future capability?

COACHING SIGNALS GENUINE CARING AND GROWS TRUST

The coaching style supports and reinforces trust through delegation. Leaders have three levers to work with to grow and maintain trust and to repair breaches. These are competence, benevolence, and integrity (see Figure 5.3).

Figure 5.3: The Three Levers of Trust

Leaders show competence by setting a compelling direction. They create enabling structures for work (such as work design, allocation of resources, and team norms).

Expert coaching by the leader conveys benevolence. It signals genuine caring and support. The more people experience their leader as caring and supportive, the deeper the trust. Through coaching, team members provide input and suggestions, and this helps them feel valued and appreciated. Only about one-fifth of people feel that they get feedback from their boss that helps them to do better work. About the same proportion feel they are managed in a way that motivates them to do outstanding work.

When people perceive their leaders to be benevolent, they are more likely to reciprocate. They work harder for longer and are more likely to go above and beyond what's required. Air cover is a key part of support. When team members encounter difficulties or challenges, leaders support and protect them. Team members will know that you "have their backs." Later, difficulties can be debriefed as learning opportunities rather than mistakes.

Finally, integrity means being accountable by doing what you say you will do, treating people fairly, and having values in common.

THINK LIKE
A COACH

Cognitive flexibility is like a kaleidoscope, which creates many patterns with the same pieces. Coaches have the curiosity to turn the scope to see new patterns. They can give up existing patterns. They know that there are endless possibilities.

You can be flexible without your thinking becoming fractured or fused if you stay present in the moment, open to experience. Figure 6.1 helps to explain this.

Figure 6.1: Perspective and Cognitive Flexibility

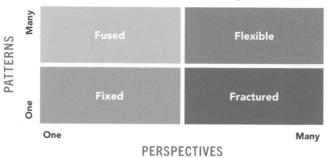

Cognitive flexibility is important in coaching in two ways.

First, it helps you as coach to stay present. You suspend your ego, remaining open to what the person you are coaching says and does. You hear and appreciate their position. You seek to understand their story from their viewpoint. You keep your own views in check.

Second, you develop it in others as you coach. You model flexibility. Increasing your flexibility is a way to help your coachee do the same. They become self-generating and better able to manage their own ongoing development.

HOW TO FLEXIBLY POSITION YOUR THINKING

Seeing things from others' points of view is like removing a set of blinders—whole new vistas can be seen. One way to do this is to be able to flexibly move between first, second, and third positions. These are three key perspectives from which to pay attention to information.

EACH POSITION REPRESENTS A WAY TO VIEW THE WORLD FROM A DIFFERENT PERSPECTIVE (SEE FIGURE 6.2):

▸ **In first position (I),** your attention is focused on your own subjective experience.

▸ **In second position (You),** your attention is focused on another person's view of the world (including how they view you).

▸ **In third position (We),** your attention is focused on neutral observation.

Figure 6.2: Three Different Perspectives

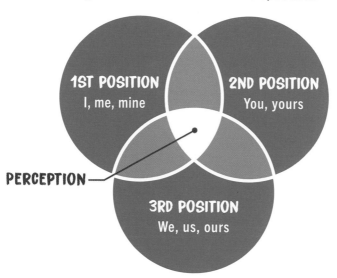

First Position

In first position, you experience the world through your own eyes. First position focuses your attention on your inner experience, on how you think and feel about your ideas and experiences. From first position, you focus on you.

First position relies on language that refers things back to you:

- I feel…
- I think…
- My opinion about that is…
- I think you are wrong about that…
- What I would do in that situation is…

Operating predominantly from first position restricts your ability to form relationships. You focus on what matters to you to the exclusion of what matters to others. Being in first position reduces your ability to understand others. Someone who spends most of their time in first position is generally seen as egotistical or insensitive. You rely on your perceptions of *another* in your engagement. This may or may not be accurate.

Second Position

Second position is essential in building and maintaining relationships. It represents empathy, putting yourself in another's shoes. From second position, you understand how someone else experiences the world and how they experience you. You check your assumptions about what the person is thinking and feeling.

From second position, you use language that refers things to the other person:

- ▸ I notice you are…
- ▸ I hear you say…
- ▸ That seems to suggest you are…
- ▸ I don't know if this is right, but you seem…

Operating predominantly in second position means that you spend too much time paying attention to others and you may lose yourself. Someone stuck in second position is generally seen as a caretaker or rescuer.

Third Position

From third position, you experience the situation as an external, neutral observer—even if you are a participant. You watch what happens. You understand it without experiencing the direct emotions of those involved (including yourself).

In third position, you use language that is impersonal:

- ▸ It seems that…
- ▸ We might assume…
- ▸ People sometimes…

Operating predominantly in third position means that you develop only superficial relationships. You lose your own sense of self. Someone stuck in third position is generally seen as detached, impersonal, and cold.

Imagine if someone shouts at you or is angry with you. If you respond in first position, you take it personally. You respond with your emotions and may feel overwhelmed or shout back. Either is unlikely to be the best response. First position is the least helpful to manage relational or emotional situations.

If you respond in second position, you are likely

to notice the other's anger or distress. Locating the emotion in them helps you avoid reacting to it. You maintain your calm and engage without matching the emotion. You might respond by naming the anger. You might suggest ways to have a discussion to resolve the issue. Second position is the most helpful position in this instance.

If you respond in third position, you are likely to observe the emotion. You will comment on the dynamics of your interaction. You may say something like "It seems that you are quite upset with this. Each time we raise this issue, it seems to end up in an emotional shouting match. What do we need to change?" Taking this position will be most helpful if it follows a response that creates empathy.

MANAGING ATTENTION

Overall, your attention is divided among the three positions. Being aware of how you control your attention allows you to organize it to achieve the outcomes you seek. As a leader, first position should receive the least amount of your attention—about 15 percent—as you focus less on you. Your job is to get the work done through others. About half of your attention is focused in second position. This allows you to monitor the people with whom you relate and to deal with issues as they arise. About 35 percent of your attention is in third position. You need to maintain perspective on the interactions around you to manage ideas and information and to manage the situation.

When you are actively coaching, you may find that second position takes a greater percentage of your attention—maybe as high as 75 percent—with first position back to 5 to 10 percent and third at about 10 to 15 percent.

HOW UNHOOKING YOUR THINKING HELPS YOU COACH

It's quite easy for our thoughts to "hook" us. We can become stuck in our thinking. We can't rid our minds of a particular thought. We are not able to make change or take action that we know will be useful. Instead, we get caught up in a negative loop—we're *hooked*.

Team members are the same. There will be times when you can see that their thinking is stuck. They are hooked on a thought or belief that is unhelpful for them. This is very normal. It's pretty much what all minds do. Our minds judge, compare, and tend to predict the worst.

When this happens, our thinking is fused. It becomes a problem when the feeling of being stuck evokes a negative reaction. These are the hooks that hold back change: they are the inner voice telling us "I'm not good enough," "I'll fail," "Nobody likes me," "I'll look foolish," "I don't deserve it." Instead of being thoughts that we have, our thoughts have us. We are hooked.

As coach, it can be helpful to identify the thoughts that have you. These hooks affect how we talk about ourselves. They become fused with our identities and the stories we tell about ourselves. They become boundaries that may have protected us in the past, but now they prevent our growth.

RECOGNIZING YOUR OWN HOOKS

Anna, a highly accomplished young leader, as her current goal chose to liberate herself from her internal voices. She wanted to be able to hear her own self.

She replayed conflicting parental voices. One was a highly critical "you will never be any good," and the other was "take risks, strive hard, achieve." The internal conflict reflected her current impasse and helped her to liberate herself from it. For her, these internal voices were quite intrusive. Coaching allowed her to transform her confusion and discomfort into a catalyst for her growth. Having made progress here, she was able to focus on the career and other leadership goals that brought her to coaching.

For others, recognizing that such thoughts are happening is enough. Bringing patterns to the surface to identify specific criticisms opens them up to examination.

What's important is how workable your thoughts are for you. Respond to your inner thoughts and criticisms in terms of their workability (how helpful they are) rather than worrying about how true they are.

As uncomfortable as it is, clarifying and examining critical internal voices allows us to make choices about their value. Then we can shift the level of influence they have over us.

When you feel hooked or pulled and a negative emotion results, take a pause. Note the feeling. What triggered it? What did your mind say or do that hooked you? How did your behavior change when you were hooked? Did you manage to unhook yourself? How?

HOW TO BE LESS BIASED

Sometimes, it feels hard enough to work on the hooks and cognitive challenges we know we have. But there are others that we remain unaware of. Decisions are often driven by thoughts and feelings of which we are unaware. Yet they profoundly influence the way we engage and with whom. As coach, you need to become more aware of when unconscious beliefs might limit how you engage with particular individuals. That way, you can mitigate against the beliefs.

It is possible to minimize the negative influence unconscious thinking has on decisions, including decisions on who we coach, how we coach them, and how much effort we put into coaching them. Our minds are like icebergs. A small but powerful fraction of our thinking is available to our conscious minds (the tip of the iceberg). Despite popular belief, most of our decisions aren't made at the conscious level through rational, logical processes.

Unconscious associations influence responses that are more difficult to control. These include nonverbal responses or responses that are automatic and people don't try to control. Unconscious beliefs influence us most when:

▸ we don't have clear decision-making criteria,
▸ we don't have or take the time to deliberate on our decisions,

▸ information is ambiguous so it's not clear how it helps us make the decision, and

▸ there is no open scrutiny of the decision.

Under these circumstances, our decision-making may be biased. The following are biases that occur when unconscious beliefs influence decision-making:

▸ **Affinity bias:** We like people who are most like us, those with whom we share an affinity such as gender, culture, or style, and we favor them over others. To what extent might affinity bias who you coach?

▸ **Expectancy bias:** We create expectations and interpret others' behavior using people categories. Professor Nalini Joshi avoids wearing a black suit to business functions. She is often mistaken for waitstaff despite being one of Australia's foremost mathematics scholars. A largely white culture expects a woman with brown skin to be in a support/ service role rather than the keynote speaker. How do your associations influence the expectations you have of people from different cultures?

▸ **Confirmation bias:** We pay attention to behavior that confirms people categories. We disregard information that disputes them. We may pay attention when women appear unconfident but disregard it when women appear confident. We seek out information that confirms our stereotypes and ignore or reinterpret it when it does not.

▸ **Directive bias:** We use gender schema to direct the context so that gender-consistent information is elicited. For example, we are more likely to ask women about their children and men about their work. Conversations at work with women about their families reinforce their role in child-rearing. A colleague may ask someone who does not have white skin where they were born and be embarrassed when they answer "Texas" with a broad Southern twang. How much might this affect the choices you make when you coach?

▸ **Self-selection bias:** Women's own biases cause them to opt out of opportunities. For example, women may apply harsher judgment about their suitability for promotion. As coach, what might you do to help them to more accurately assess their capabilities?

Here are five strategies you can employ to make better decisions and to break free of your hooks and biases:

1 **Slow down and focus your attention.** Associations are more likely to come into play when decisions are made quickly and intuitively. Be mindfully present and aware when you are making decisions about your team members. Take the time to consider a variety of options, weighing the costs and benefits of each.

2   **Cultivate empathy and connection.** Focus first on relationship, then on task.

3   **Question yourself.** Question your motives, assumptions, and choices. What's another way to see this? What further information do you need? What assumptions are you making? What assumptions can you see this person making that limit their choices?

4   **Review multiple perspectives.** Take a broader frame of reference, and discuss options with people who think differently from you. How do others see this? Try some what-if scenarios. Take the opposite perspective and ask why not.

5   **Commit to action.** Identify what gets in your way of fair thinking. Keep focused on improving yourself.

WARM IT UP LIKE A COACH

The four coaching basics support coaching conversations, no matter their purpose, whether they are everyday, business-as-usual, feedback conversations, or even challenging conversations. In addition to developing rapport with your team and always ensuring you are actively listening to your star players, there are two key tricks you can use as a coach to ensure success. These two coaching basics are:

1   Create psychological safety.

2   Ask open questions to expand the conversation and maintain the coaching purpose.

When you learn to juggle, it can be hard work to get all the balls moving to the right rhythm and to keep them all in the air. It's helpful to start with one ball, then add the second, mastering each step one at a time. Starting off with the whole task is too daunting. You wouldn't just throw all the balls in the air and hope to start juggling! Learning to have new kinds of conversations is the same.

WHY PSYCHOLOGICAL SAFETY MATTERS TO COACHING

Psychological safety provides a strong foundation for a great coaching relationship. When leaders actively pay attention to psychological safety, they set up a context that allows team members to bring their full selves in.

Psychological safety describes perceptions of the consequences of taking interpersonal risks in a particular context. It facilitates the willing contribution of ideas and actions to a shared enterprise.

Being fully present in a team can be challenging for some team members. Wisely, people won't risk the challenge of swinging out on the trapeze if there isn't a safety net. Likewise, in teamwork they won't risk the challenge of bringing their full selves in if there isn't the right level of psychological safety. Your job as the coach is to create the safety net and maintain it in good order.

How to Create Psychological Safety

For people to feel safe at work, you need to meet five important human needs:

1   **I matter.** My being here has value.

2   **I belong.** I feel like I am a part of this team.

3   **I'm enabled.** I have what I need to contribute to the team.

4   **I contribute.** What I do makes a difference to the team.

5   **I'm respected.** You recognize me for who I am.

Establishing a set of ground rules can help you pay explicit attention to these needs, and you can involve your team in the process. Psychological safety creates a climate that increases the chances of learning behavior. It supports people to engage in collaborative work and undertake new activities. They are more likely to seek help, experiment, and discuss errors or mistakes. This climate is a strong foundation for coaching.

HOW OPEN QUESTIONS EXPAND COACHING CONVERSATIONS

Questions that expand thinking and open lines of inquiry are key tools for good coaching. They allow the coachee to take ownership of the conversation's direction and ideally expand their thinking. Open questions prevent telling, directing, answering, and knowing, all of which close off thinking.

Questions work like funnels in conversations. If you start with closed questions, you'll only get contraction. Open questions create expansion (see Figure 7.1).

Figure 7.1: The Effect of Types of Questions

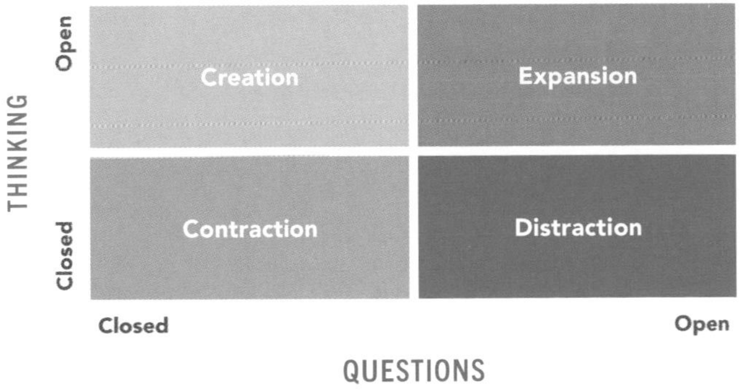

Closed and leading questions offer little opportunity for growth and development. Closed questions elicit only yes, no, or maybe responses. They shut down possibilities. And once answered, another question has to be asked immediately. A succession of closed questions can feel very much like an interrogation.

CLOSED QUESTIONS START WITH:

- Have…?
- Will…?
- Did…?
- Must…?

Leading questions may initially seem as if they are going to be open questions, but they are not. They end with one suggestion that requires agreement or disagreement.

LEADING QUESTIONS START WITH:

- What about doing…?

▸ How about trying…?

▸ Might you consider the possibility…?

Open questions allow the respondent the space to answer the question in their own way.

OPEN QUESTIONS START WITH:

▸ What…?

▸ Where…?

▸ How…?

▸ Who…?

▸ When…?

"Why" is an open question but needs judicious use, as it can lead to defensiveness. There is usually another way to ask a why question as an open question. "Why did you…?" might be better expressed as "What thinking led you to that conclusion?"

PART 3

COACH

PLAY IT LIKE
A COACH

Don't use a coaching approach with your team members solely for performance management or in structured meetings. Provide micro-coaching in everyday moments.

Used in this way, coaching has the spontaneity of a jazz band. In a jazz band, when the musicians become attuned to one another and to the moment, they adapt and respond in their playing and their call and answer as the mood takes them. The music can take many iterations rather than relying on one predetermined score.

One of the impediments to managers using coaching more is that they claim they don't have the time. I challenge this thinking because it contains within it a fundamental misconception of what it means to be a leader. What is the role of the leader? Is it to do? Or is it to support others to do? The primary responsibility of leaders is to get the work done through others. Coaching is most potent and easiest to do in day-to-day conversations.

A coaching style changes the nature of conversations. By focusing at the level of conversation, coaching is simpler and easier.

BE OPEN TO COACHING CONVERSATIONS AT ANY TIME

Coaching conversations can occur at any time. Leaders should be attuned to openings for exploring development. One of the openings you create when you focus on creating coaching moments is for development.

Unless you're in a crisis, there is always time to focus on development.

For example, if your team member approaches you and asks you a question, you are most likely to answer with a solution. Rather than jumping straight to that solution, try pausing. Whether or not you know the answer becomes immaterial (at least for this conversation!). Instead, ask questions, such as the following:

▸ What have you already done?

▸ What have you thought of but haven't yet tried?

▸ What information do you need to be able to answer the question yourself

▸ How did that work?

▸ Who do you know who does this well? What would they do?

▸ What would you do if you had different resources?

▸ What have you thought of doing next?

▸ Who else is involved?

These questions elicit more information about the context. They can help clarify what the options are, and they can help identify new options. They can help shape what will work and what might not work.

It's asking questions and the questions we ask that make the difference.

Rather than viewing coaching as something to do from time to time, see it as less of a prescription. Leaders should ask themselves in every moment not whether or not to coach but *what to coach for.*

FULLY EXPLORE LINES OF QUESTIONS

Coaching focuses on making a high-quality experience for the person being coached. One tactic for doing this is to stay with lines of questions. As coach, make sure you explore each line of questioning, taking it to its conclusion. Avoid asking random questions based on momentary thoughts or your own interests.

Following question lines is like a flock of geese flying in formation. Each one notices the position of the others and uses their updraft/downdraft to fly in formation. As coach, each question you ask or response you make should align with the direction the coachee has taken.

While geese make this look effortless, it's not so easy in conversations. You will need to put aside your ego and your interests and listen carefully. Ask yourself these questions:

- Have I fully explored point X, or is there further information I can elicit?

- In what direction is this conversation going?
- Are we moving in a particular direction to develop a deeper understanding?
- When is it time to shift attention to another thread?

As you keep the line of questions in mind, be aware of when the coachee sets up their own diversions. Is the openness unfamiliar or too challenging? Perhaps they don't know the answer or are distracted. While the focus is on them and the question line is theirs, make sure they too stick with it as makes best sense.

Remember:

- Pay attention to the coachee by minimizing the distractions in your head.
- Listen to the answers from your coachee.
- Think about the follow-up question to their response.
- Follow a thread until it reaches its conclusion.

ACTIVITY

1. What did you observe about yourself as you coached? What learning did you take from your observation?

2. What feedback have you received on your coaching?

3. What will you undertake to do in the same way, and what would you do differently next time you coach? As you become more comfortable coaching, review your progress on a monthly basis.

4. Consider how your practice is evolving. What is becoming easier to do? What have you avoided doing?

5. What's your relative balance of coaching in the moment versus coaching in dedicated conversations? How well does the balance work for you?

6. How are your team members responding to coaching? What's changing for them? How does that make it easier or harder for you to coach them?

IMPROVE THE PLAY
WITH FEEDBACK

Feedback is a word that strikes fear into many people, so much so that we've mostly learned to avoid it. Feedback is often not given well or not offered at all. In the absence of explicit feedback on how we are doing, we either keep doing what we've always done—irrespective of how effective it has been—or rely on our own feedback to ourselves. Neither is optimal for growth and development.

In many organizations, feedback is seldom given, so when you offer to give feedback to someone, they may become anxious or suspicious or try to avoid hearing it.

Why? Because we've mixed up a couple of simple things. We've tended to equate feedback with criticism. We see it as always about the negative, about what's wrong. And that gets in the way of good feedback, which is an important part of coaching.

When coaching, we want to focus on what to improve and what to generate. We need a way to notice where improvement is possible or needed. We need a way to notice where the gaps are and where the opportunities for growth are. As coach, your focus is always on improvement. Regular feedback is an opportunity to improve the play.

To incorporate feedback into coaching takes courage, generativity, and caring by the coach. These mindsets create a positive framework for giving feedback (see Figure 9.1). There are three especially important areas where giving regular feedback will be of great benefit:

1 **Increasing current strengths:** This is often overlooked, but it is a very powerful and positive focus for feedback. How could this person be better at what they are already good at? If someone is a great communicator with internal stakeholders, how might they grow those strengths to other areas? Are there opportunities to engage with external stakeholders?

2 **Improving current performance:** This is not a performance conversation! This is an opportunity to grow, to tweak the edges, to transfer skills to new contexts, to develop mastery.

3 **Developing capability needed in the future:** How might you moderate the enthusiasm this person has for getting things done to help them take a more strategic perspective? How can they develop that now in readiness for promotion into a more senior role? How can they develop capability for and

demonstrate skills in preparation for moving into their next role? How might their job change in the future? What different skills might be needed?

Figure 9.1: The Positive Feedback Framework

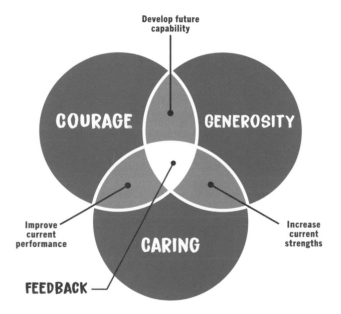

Sometimes, feedback will focus on what's not working. This reshapes behavior that is unhelpful or interferes with progress. More often, feedback should focus on what's going right. This helps reinforce the right behavior and develop mastery. *Feedback isn't criticism, and criticism isn't feedback.*

Most people don't give feedback, they give criticism. No wonder it doesn't go down so well!

Criticism is judgmental. It is you interpreting me—from your lens. It keeps control in the hands of the critic. It usually comes with an agenda. It's not coaching, because it reduces options rather than increases them.

STEPS FOR GIVING GOOD FEEDBACK

You can become more comfortable with the process of giving feedback if you use a clear, step-by-step structure. Here is a clear map to make it easier to navigate the tough territory of feedback. This is a more defined conversation structure than that outlined earlier in chapter 8 but keeps the spirit of the coaching process going. Make sure that you focus on building the relationship and that you explore plenty of possibilities.

THERE ARE FIVE KEY INGREDIENTS FOR CLEAR FEEDBACK:

1 It has a clear business purpose.

2 It is based on observation.

3 It is specific.

4 It is timely.

5 It will improve performance.

ACCEPT ALL RESPONSES TO FEEDBACK

Despite good planning and execution, you may find that your feedback is not met with hugs and roses or even with a simple thank-you. It is easier to give feedback when there is a receptive listener. It is more challenging if your feedback meets with resistance of some kind. But by accepting all responses to feedback, even outright rejection, it is possible to foster acceptance and to embed a culture of feedback.

Don't push back against any resistance. Open up the opportunity to have a conversation to deepen your understanding. Move with the push, and take it into a dance. What's the source of the resistance? How does the resistance help you to give better feedback? What else do you need to do or to know?

If you're developing a new emphasis on feedback, then expect resistance and skepticism. What would be in your team member's mind? "Is this a one-off?" "Is this something I can avoid?" "It won't last…"

Keep in your mind these questions: "How will I stay calm?" "How can I better understand the resistance?" "What's another way to say this?"

Our usual response to resistance is to push back.

We can be caught off guard. We lose our balance and feel surprised, dominated, defensive, resentful, angry, or hurt. We match the resistance.

Resistance isn't usually an end point. It's a way station on the path to acceptance. As the coach, you have the opportunity to take a generous mindset. As you develop your understanding of how the path of resistance works, pay more attention to the responses you receive. Even though the initial response to tough feedback might be resistance, with patience you may move through to acceptance. Make sure you are in charge of the direction you are going. Identify where you are at on the resistance and acceptance path (see Figure 9.2). Keep the conversation focused on moving forward. How can you provide support to help movement along the path?

Figure 9.2: The Feedback Acceptance Path

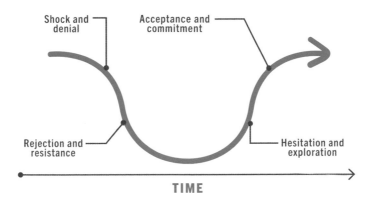

Resistance can be caused by insecurity, lack of knowledge, and fear of change. You can help people move through their own personal cycle of change in response to feedback and the organization's broader change programs. Notice how people respond to change, and adapt your responses so that they can move forward.

WHEN IT COMES TO THE CRUNCH

From time to time, there will be a need to have a crunch conversation. Sometimes, a feedback conversation might be particularly challenging for you. Perhaps you want to address some ongoing tensions or deal with conflict. You may need to give a tough performance review or say no to someone in need. You may need to confront disrespectful behavior, disagree with a majority view, or ask for a pay raise. For some of us, these conversations can be quite challenging to face.

A crunch conversation is one that requires some courage; it's anything you find hard to talk about. Crunch conversations change the tension or "stuck-ness" between people. Their purpose is to take the relationship to a new and better place.

Left to themselves, small embers of discord and dissatisfaction can smolder and flare up. You can become consumed by putting out little fires. If you act to put out the little fires, you may evoke fear, but you are extinguishing the flames and preventing a major burn.

Self-manage your own response to conflict so that you avoid less and overreact less. Better manage your own fight-or-flight response. And always in coaching mode help others to better manage their responses. As Nelson Mandela's wisdom reminds us, "I learned that courage was not the absence of fear, but the triumph over it."

Identify When a Crunch Conversation Is Needed

If you know what triggers you, you can move quickly to have a crunch conversation that will recover the relationship. By knowing your triggers, you can also manage them better and avoid feeling conflict. If you are aware of what your triggers are, you can become better at keeping your own safety catch on.

CHEER LIKE
A COACH

As a coach, you have the opportunity to make a big difference to the motivation of your team members. Cheer their progress and notice the difference it makes.

The single most important factor in engaging people in their jobs is the perception that they are making progress in meaningful work. When people experience a sense of progress, they are more intrinsically motivated. Their interest in and enjoyment of the work itself becomes the strongest motivator. Even quite small progress steps can make a big difference.

So how can you create motivation?

Here is a list of five motivators that came out of a survey of managers from companies around the world:

1 Recognition for good work

2 Tangible incentives such as pay

3 Support for making progress in the work

4 Interpersonal support

5 Having clear goals

Which of these five do you believe has the biggest effect on motivation?

Recognition for good work ranked number one according to the managers in the survey. While recognition does boost motivation, data shows that making progress does so to a far greater extent. Support for making progress was answered as number one by only 5 percent of managers in the survey cited above. What we believe motivates people isn't what actually motivates them day to day. Cheering matters. *But it's how you cheer that matters most.*

HOW YOU CAN IMPROVE MOTIVATION FOR YOUR TEAM

How can you use your deeper knowledge of motivation to improve performance? There are three important ways to affect momentum for a team: a sense of progress, catalysts, and nourishers. A coaching style allows you to develop a deeper understanding of what will help motivate each particular individual in your team. You can promote progress, provide catalysts, and nourish your team members (see Figure 10.1).

Figure 10.1: Ways to Improve Inner Work-Life

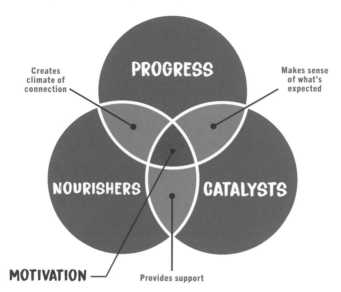

THE PROGRESS PRINCIPLE

Progress triggers positive emotions like satisfaction, happiness, joy, and gladness. Making headway on meaningful work improves inner work-life and boosts long-term performance. It creates a positive loop: positive inner work-life creates progress, which creates positive inner work-life.

So as a part of any work, it's important that you provide feedback, that you notice the efforts and results of your team's work. How do they know they're making progress? What feedback do you give them on their progress? How often do you do this? How good are you at noticing and celebrating their progress?

As noted previously, bad is stronger than good; the power of the negative far outweighs that of the positive. The power of setbacks to increase frustration is more than three times as strong as the power of progress to decrease frustration. Do you notice when your team members experience that sense of a setback and take action to help them to recover from it? Do you pay attention to how you convey news of a setback?

CATALYSTS

Catalysts facilitate timely, creative, and high-quality work. There are seven major catalysts in the workplace:

1   Having clear and meaningful goals: *I know what to do.*

2   Allowing autonomy: *I can get on with my work without undue oversight.*

3   Providing sufficient resources: *I have the resources I need to do my work.*

4   Giving enough (but not too much) time to get work done: *I can get the work done in the time expected.*

5   Help with the work from managers and colleagues: *I know I will get help when I ask for it.*

6   Learning from problems and successes: *I keep learning and improving.*

7   Allowing ideas to flow: *I can contribute my ideas.*

There are three main ways for you to shape the availability of catalysts for your team. First, you can show good consideration for people and their ideas. Second, you can make sure systems and procedures are well coordinated. Third, you can ensure clear, honest, respectful, and free-flowing communication occurs.

Some of the failures of leadership that you should avoid include:

- creating ambiguity
- unclear, overlapping, or duplicated accountabilities
- telling different people different reasons for tasks
- encouraging people two layers down to speak directly to you about problems
- not being aware of and/or not managing team tensions
- underestimating the likelihood and significance of interpersonal problems
- not noticing erosion of trust

The overall organizational climate also shapes the availability of catalysts. Unclear goals, too much control, and insufficient resources inhibit progress and motivation. If leaders remove these barriers, people's own intrinsic motivation will get the job done.

NOURISHERS

You nourish the inner work-life of your team members when you recognize, encourage, and support them. Help them resolve interpersonal conflict. Provide opportunities for people to know one another better and to celebrate and have fun. These all nourish the human connection.

NOURISHMENT COMES FROM:

▸ showing respect

▸ giving encouragement

▸ providing emotional support

▸ growing affiliation

A lack of attention to nourishers can mean that there are spillover effects, with conflict and contagion from bad moods spreading. This contributes to a toxic climate in the workplace. Move quickly to contain the spread.

If you are coaching your team members, you will be nourishing them too.

AFTERWORD

Leaders model coaching in an "everyone coaches" culture. Before I leave you, I wanted to share some further examples of how leading like a coach works in practice and to include some final advice to ensure that when you move toward a coaching model in your team or your organization, you have the best chance of making it a success.

A coaching culture balances the need to deliver

results now with the need to deliver results in the future.

A coaching style reinforces a flexible culture that is guided by purpose and learning, where people welcome change rather than stability. They care about the future and are open and agile. Coaching embodies these features. This creates an affinity between the means and the end: you coach a coaching culture into reality.

You have a coaching culture if:

1   Senior leaders believe in coaching and coach.

2   Leaders look for opportunities to help others learn.

3   Leaders ask open questions rather than telling the solution.

4   People willingly give and receive feedback.

5   People have honest and open conversations.

If coaching isn't a priority for managers, then you know you don't have a coaching culture in your organization. The best coaching cultures are those where leaders use a coaching style with their teams. When leaders are coaching and their teams are learning that this is how we do things here, a coaching style becomes pervasive. Anyone can coach, anytime.

Team members can take the opportunity to have coaching conversations with their bosses, peers can use the coaching style as they engage with one another, and so on. Coaching behaviors in these contexts take a conversational form. The responsibility is to maintain and articulate a developmental, action-oriented frame of reference.

A coaching culture supports leaders who coach. As coach, you focus on "filling everyone else's bucket." It is as important to keep yourself replenished. In a coaching culture, support, encouragement, and replenishment come from those around you. Create a circle of like-minded coaching advocates. Make a commitment to meet on a regular basis to coach one another on your own development and well-being.

A culture characterized by coaching has within it the seeds to create a sustainable, self-generating leadership legacy. By being deliberately developmental, a coaching culture grows future leaders as it empowers and develops current leaders.

If you have learned nothing else, I hope you now realize that it is not just leaders who coach. Anyone in any role at any level can also take a coaching approach. This creates an "everyone coaches" culture where anyone can lead, where the tools of success are in your hands to create a winning team and culture *today*.

Are you ready, Coach?

ACKNOWLEDGMENTS

Lead Like a Coach would not have been possible without the generosity and openness of the many people I've had the privilege to coach. Coaching you has given me a rich experience, which has shaped my own development as a coach as well as given me the impetus to write this book. Thank you.

Being a part of the Thought Leaders Business School community motivated me to write this book. I would not have done it so well or so quickly without the intellectual elegance and rigor of the TLBS process. Special thanks to Kieran Flanagan for working through the title with me. It provided clarity and focus. That helped me to clarify my purpose for the book, and writing it then became a pleasure.

Big thank-you to Peter for love, coffee, and, importantly, help with those occasional, inevitable technical crises.

I could not have had better support turning the manuscript into the final product than I've received from Lesley Williams and the team at Major Street Publishing. Thank you so much for your wise and efficient support.

ABOUT THE
AUTHOR

DR. KAREN MORLEY helps leaders realize their full potential. She helps leaders meet the challenges of growing engaged, motivated, productive people who love their work, respect their bosses, and are proud of their organizations.

Karen appreciates that the work of leadership is challenging. Her career has been devoted to working with leaders to influence their development. She continues to admire those exceptional leaders whom everyone loves to work with and who get great results. Her goal is to help spread a bit of this magic to all leaders. We need to lighten the weight of leadership and make it more enjoyable and fulfilling.

Karen is an experienced executive coach and greatly enjoys coaching individual leaders. She has coached leaders at organizations as diverse as the Australian Institute of Company Directors (AICD), Allens, BHP Billiton, Broadspectrum, CBA, Coles, CSL, CUB, Downer, ExxonMobil, GCC, KPMG, Latitude Financial, Lendlease, L'Oréal, Lumleys, Medibank, Melbourne Airport, Melbourne Water, Monash Health, Officeworks, Orica, QBE, RACV, Rural Finance, Target, UGL, University of Melbourne, and VisionStream.

Karen brings broad experiences, top professional credentials, and a variety of perspectives. She's a registered psychologist with a desire to align what leaders do with the available evidence for what works. Besides being an executive coach and leadership developer, Karen has held executive roles in government and higher education, and her approach is informed by her experience in these roles. Along the way, she completed a doctorate in leadership, published *Gender Balanced Leadership: An Executive Guide*, and has written numerous other working and white papers. She is an honorary fellow of the University of Melbourne and a director at the Australia and New Zealand School of Government.

Karen lives in Melbourne, Australia. She chairs the board of Emerge Women and Children's Support Network, which assists women and children affected by domestic violence.

NEW! Only from Simple Truths®

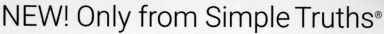
IGNITE READS
spark impact in just one hour

IGNITE READS IS A NEW SERIES OF 1-HOUR READS WRITTEN BY WORLD-RENOWNED EXPERTS!

These captivating books will help you become the best version of yourself, allowing for new opportunities in your personal and professional life. Accelerate your career and expand your knowledge with these powerful books written on today's hottest ideas.

TRENDING BUSINESS AND PERSONAL GROWTH TOPICS

 Read in an hour or less

 Leading experts and authors

 Bold design and captivating content

EXCLUSIVELY AVAILABLE ON SIMPLETRUTHS.COM

Need a training framework?
Engage your team with discussion guides and PowerPoints for training events or meetings.

Want your own branded editions?
Express gratitude, appreciation, and instill positive perceptions to staff or clients by adding your organization's logo to your edition of the book.

Add a supplemental visual experience
to any meeting, training, or event.

Contact us for special corporate discounts!
(800) 900-3427 x247 or simpletruths@sourcebooks.com

LOVED WHAT YOU READ AND WANT MORE?

Sign up today and be the FIRST to receive advance copies of Simple Truths® NEW releases written and signed by expert authors. Enjoy a complete package of supplemental materials that can help you host or lead a successful event. This high-value program will uplift you to be the best version of yourself!

— SIMPLE TRUTHS —
ELITE CLUB
ONE MONTH. ONE BOOK. ONE HOUR.

Your monthly dose of motivation, inspiration, and personal growth.